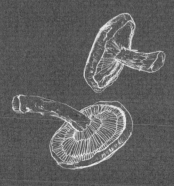

RAMEN, SOBA & UDON

RAMEN, SOBA & UDON

PLUS OTHER NOODLE DISHES

This edition published by Parragon Books Ltd in 2014 and distributed by

Parragon Inc.
440 Park Avenue South, 13th Floor
New York, NY 10016
www.parragon.com/lovefood

LOVE FOOD is an imprint of Parragon Books Ltd

ISBN 978-1-4723-6453-1

Printed in China

Project managed by Kerry Starr
New recipes written by Robin Donovan
New photography by Mike Cooper
New home economy by Lincoln Jefferson
Introduction and incidental text written by Rachel Carter
New internal illustrations by Nicola O'Byrne
Production controller: Joe Xavier

Notes for the Reader
This book uses standard kitchen measuring spoons and cups. All spoon and cup measurements are level unless otherwise indicated. Unless otherwise stated, milk is assumed to be whole, eggs are large, individual vegetables are medium, and pepper is freshly ground black pepper. Unless otherwise stated, all root vegetables should be peeled prior to using.

Garnishes, decorations, and serving suggestions are all optional and not necessarily included in the recipe ingredients or method. Any optional ingredients and seasoning to taste are not included in the nutritional analysis. The times given are only an approximate guide. Preparation times differ according to the techniques used by different people, and the cooking times may also vary from those given. Optional ingredients, variations, or serving suggestions have not been included in the time calculations.

CONTENTS

SOBA SO GOOD...

THE HISTORY OF THE NOODLE

Noodle: A very long, thin strip of pasta or similar flour paste, eaten with a sauce or in a soup.

Origin: Late eighteenth century from the German term nudel.

The exact origin of noodles seems to be clouded in mystery and has been the subject of much debate. Indeed, whole books have been devoted to the subject of this much-loved food, which is essentially a starch-based dough, sold in a variety of shapes and thicknesses, some in coils, others in bundles.

Whether the Italian merchant traveler Marco Polo was responsible for bringing noodles from China to Italy via the Silk Road remains unproven, but their evolution is an interesting one.

What seems certain is that the ancestor to the noodle was not called "noodle." In the Eastern Han Dynasty, "cake" is the original term associated with anything made with flour and water, and initially it was not formed into the string-like pieces that we think of as noodles.

In the third century AD, a Chinese dictionary refers to them as *mian pian,* or "little pieces of bread dough," and in the Hebrew Talmud of the fifth century AD there are references to a food resembling a noodle in shape made from semolina called *itrium.*

In 2002, archeologists made a fascinating discovery at the Lajia excavations near the Yellow River (or Huang He) in northwest China, where the oldest-known noodles were found. Using carbon dating, they have been placed at about 4,000 years old. They were preserved in a sealed, overturned bowl buried under ten feet of sediment. The yellow noodles were long and thin and thought to be made by hand-stretching the dough, showing a high level of culinary sophistication. Interestingly, they were found to be derived from two types of millet: foxtail and broomcorn, both of which were indigenous to China and widely cultivated 7,000 years ago.

The earliest mention of noodles dates back to a book in China's Eastern Han Dynasty between AD 25 and 200, when they were often made from wheat dough. It's thought they were a staple in the diets of many in that period.

While the Arabs, Chinese, and Italians all lay claim to noodles, it seems certain that the Italians should be credited with spreading their popularity throughout the world.

Instant noodles were first marketed in Japan in 1958, when it was discovered that drying fresh noodles and then flash-frying them prolonged their shelf life.

A BIRD IN THE HAND

TURKEY MISO SOUP

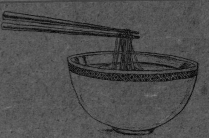

This comforting soup, enriched with miso paste, is just the thing to warm you up on a cold winter's day.

SERVES: 4　　　　**PREP TIME: 5 MINS**　　　　**COOK TIME: 25 MINS**

INGREDIENTS

8 ounces fresh udon noodles

1 tablespoon vegetable oil

1 small leek, white and light-green parts halved lengthwise and thinly sliced

10 cups turkey stock

3 carrots, sliced

1 teaspoon white pepper

4 cups halved sugar snap peas

2 cups cooked turkey meat, shredded or chopped

¼ cup white miso paste

1. Cook the noodles according to the package directions.

2. Heat the oil in a medium saucepan over medium–high heat. Add the leek and cook, stirring frequently, for 3 minutes, or until it begins to soften. Add the stock, carrots, and pepper and bring to a boil. Reduce the heat to low and simmer for 15 minutes, or until the carrots are just tender.

3. Add the sugar snap peas, turkey, and cooked noodles and simmer for 2–3 minutes, until heated through. Stir in the miso paste until it is dissolved.

4. Transfer the soup to warm bowls and serve immediately.

HERO TIPS

This soup is great to store in the freezer so that you can heat up a bowl whenever you like, but cook and add the noodles just before serving.

CHICKEN NOODLE SOUP

SERVES: 4-6   **PREP TIME: 15 MINS**   **COOK TIME: 35 MINS**

INGREDIENTS

2 skinless, boneless chicken breasts

8½ cups water

1 onion, with skin left on, cut in half

1 large garlic clove, cut in half

½-inch piece fresh ginger, peeled and sliced

4 black peppercorns, lightly crushed

4 cloves

2 star anise

1 celery stalk, chopped

6–8 baby corn, sliced

2 scallions, finely shredded

4 ounces dried rice vermicelli

1 carrot, peeled and shredded

salt and pepper, to taste

1. Put the chicken breasts and water into a saucepan and bring to a boil. Reduce the heat and simmer, skimming the surface until no more foam rises.

2. Add the onion, garlic, ginger, peppercorns, cloves, star anise, and a pinch of salt. Continue to simmer for 20 minutes, or until the chicken is tender and no longer pink when cut into.

3. Strain the chicken, reserving about 5 cups of the stock but discarding any flavoring solids. Return the reserved stock to the rinsed-out pan and add the celery, baby corn, and scallions.

4. Bring the stock to a boil and boil until the baby corn is almost tender, then add the noodles and continue boiling for 2 minutes.

5. Meanwhile, chop the chicken, add to the pan with the shredded carrot and continue cooking for about 1 minute, until the chicken is reheated and the noodles are soft. Season with salt and pepper.

6. Transfer the soup to warm bowls and serve immediately.

ROASTED DUCK SOUP WITH MUSHROOMS & EGGS

SERVES: 4   **PREP TIME: 10 MINS, PLUS SOAKING**   **COOK TIME: 50 MINS**

INGREDIENTS

½ ounce dried shiitake mushrooms

7¼ cups chicken stock or duck stock

¼ cup Chinese rice wine, dry sherry, or dry white wine

4-inch piece fresh ginger, peeled and sliced

2 tablespoons rice vinegar

2 tablespoons soy sauce

2 teaspoons sesame oil

1 cinnamon stick

1 star anise

1 teaspoon white pepper

1 teaspoon salt

2 cups shredded roasted duck (preferably dark meat)

6 ounces fresh shiitake mushrooms, sliced

6 ounces dried ramen noodles (flavoring envelope discarded, if included)

4 scallions, sliced diagonally into 1-inch pieces

4 eggs

chili oil, to garnish

1. Soak the mushrooms in hot water for 30 minutes. Drain, reserving the liquid, and slice.

2. Combine the stock, wine, mushroom soaking liquid, ginger, vinegar, soy sauce, sesame oil, cinnamon stick, star anise, pepper, and salt in a large saucepan. Bring to a simmer, then reduce the heat to low and simmer for 20 minutes. Strain the stock and discard the ginger slices. Return the stock, star anise, and cinnamon stick to the pan. Bring back to a simmer and add the duck meat, the reserved soaked dried mushrooms, and the fresh mushrooms. Simmer for an additional 20 minutes, or until the mushrooms are tender. Remove the cinnamon stick and star anise, increase the heat, and bring the soup to a boil.

3. Add the noodles and cook, breaking them up with a spoon as needed, for about 3 minutes, or until tender. Stir in the scallions.

4. To cook the eggs, fill a medium saucepan halfway with water and bring to a boil over high heat. Reduce the heat to low and carefully crack the eggs into the water. Cook for 4 minutes.

5. Ladle the soup into warm bowls and top each with an egg. Garnish with a few drops of chili oil and serve immediately.

CHINESE CHICKEN SALAD

SERVES: 4　　　　**PREP TIME: 20 MINS**　　　　**COOK TIME: 10 MINS**

INGREDIENTS

3 skinless, boneless chicken
breasts (1 pound in total),
cut into bite-size pieces

2 teaspoons soy sauce

¼ teaspoon white pepper

2 tablespoons peanut oil,
plus extra for deep-frying

2 ounces thin rice noodles

½ head Chinese greens,
thinly sliced diagonally

3 scallions, green parts
included, sliced diagonally

½ cup almonds with skin,
sliced lengthwise

sesame seeds, to garnish
(optional)

DRESSING

⅓ cup olive oil

3 tablespoons rice vinegar

3 tablespoons soy sauce

a few drops sesame oil

salt and pepper, to taste

1. Sprinkle the chicken with the soy sauce and white pepper. To make the dressing, whisk the ingredients together in a bowl until well blended.

2. Heat a wok over high heat, then add the peanut oil. Stir-fry the chicken for 4–5 minutes, until brown. Drain on paper towels and let cool. Wipe out the wok.

3. Pour enough peanut oil for deep-frying into the wok. Heat to 350-375°F, or until a cube of bread browns in 30 seconds, then fry a few noodles at a time until puffed up and crisp. Remove and drain on paper towels.

4. Arrange the Chinese greens in a shallow serving dish. Place the noodles in a pile on top of the greens on one side of the dish. Arrange the chicken, scallions, and almonds in the remaining space. Whisk the dressing again and pour it over the salad. Garnish with the sesame seeds, if using. Serve immediately.

DUCK & CRISPY RAMEN NOODLE SALAD

SERVES: 4   **PREP TIME: 20 MINS**   **COOK TIME: 15 MINS**

INGREDIENTS

4 ounces dried ramen noodles (flavoring envelope discarded, if included)

2 duck breasts, halved (about 6 ounces each)

1 cup peanut oil

salt and pepper, to taste

2 tablespoons sliced toasted almonds, to garnish

DRESSING

juice of 1 lime

2 tablespoons white miso paste

1 tablespoon low-sodium soy sauce

1 tablespoon rice vinegar

1 teaspoon grated fresh ginger

¼ cup vegetable oil

1 teaspoon sesame oil

SALAD

1 small butterhead lettuce, torn into bite-size pieces

4 clementines, peeled and sectioned

1 red jalapeño chile, seeded and finely diced

1 avocado, diced

2 tablespoons sliced toasted almonds

1. Preheat the oven to 400°F. Line a plate with paper towels.

2. Cook the noodles according to the package directions. Drain and arrange in small clumps on the prepared plate and set aside to dry.

3. To cook the duck, heat a large, ovenproof skillet over medium heat. Pat the duck breasts dry and season with salt and pepper. Using a sharp knife, score the skin, making four to six slashes across the top of each breast, being careful not to cut into the meat. When the pan is hot, add the duck breasts, skin-side down, and cook for 5–6 minutes, or until most of the fat is rendered and the skin is brown and crisp. Turn and cook for 2 minutes on the other side, until just beginning to brown. Turn the breasts again and place the pan in the preheated oven. Roast for 7–9 minutes, or until a meat thermometer registers 130°F when inserted into the thickest part of the meat. Remove from the oven and let rest for at least 5 minutes before slicing. Slice across the grain into ¼-inch-thick slices.

4. To make the crispy noodles, line a plate with paper towels. Put the oil in a small saucepan and heat over high heat until just beginning to smoke. Using tongs, add the noodles, one clump at a time,

and cook for about 20 seconds, until golden brown. Turn and cook on the other side for an additional 15–20 seconds, until golden brown. Transfer to the prepared plate to drain.

5. To make the dressing, whisk together the first five ingredients in a small bowl. Add the vegetable oil and sesame oil and whisk until combined and emulsified.

6. To assemble, toss together the salad ingredients in a large bowl. Drizzle ¼ cup of the dressing over the salad and toss to coat. Divide the salad among the plates and top each with several slices of duck, sprinkle with the almonds, and drizzle with a little more dressing. Add the noodles and serve immediately.

THAI CHICKEN & SOBA NOODLE SALAD

SERVES: 4   **PREP TIME: 15 MINS**   **COOK TIME: 10 MINS**

INGREDIENTS

8 ounces dried soba noodles

2½ cups shredded cooked chicken

1½ cups shredded cabbage

1 cucumber, peeled, seeded, and cut into matchsticks

1 red bell pepper, seeded and cut into matchsticks

3 scallions, thinly sliced, and ½ cup crushed roasted unsalted peanuts, to garnish

DRESSING

juice of 1 lime

1 tablespoon Thai fish sauce

1 tablespoon packed light brown sugar

2 tablespoons smooth peanut butter

1 garlic clove, finely chopped

1–2 small hot red chiles, seeded and finely chopped

3 tablespoons vegetable oil

¼ cup chopped fresh cilantro leaves

¼ cup chopped fresh mint leaves

1. Cook the noodles according to the package directions. Drain and rinse with cold water. Set aside to cool completely.

2. To make the dressing, combine the lime juice, fish sauce, sugar, peanut butter, garlic, and chiles in a small bowl and whisk to mix well. Whisk in the oil until well combined and emulsified. Stir in the cilantro and mint.

3. Combine the cooked noodles, chicken, cabbage, cucumber, and red bell pepper in a large bowl and toss to combine. Add the dressing and toss again to coat well. Garnish with scallions and peanuts and serve.

CHICKEN CHOW MEIN

This classic Chinese stir-fry is a familiar takeout favorite. Cooked at home, you can add any vegetables that you desire, making it not only delicious but adaptable.

SERVES: 4   **PREP TIME: 5-10 MINS**   **COOK TIME: 15 MINS**

INGREDIENTS

8 ounces dried medium Chinese egg noodles

2 tablespoons sunflower oil

2 cups cooked chicken breasts, shredded

1 garlic clove, finely chopped

1 red bell pepper, thinly sliced

4 ounces shiitake mushrooms, sliced

6 scallions, sliced

1 cup bean sprouts

3 tablespoons soy sauce

1 tablespoon sesame oil

1. Cook the noodles as per the package directions. Drain well and set aside.

2. Heat a wok over medium heat, then add the oil. Add the shredded chicken, garlic, red bell pepper, mushrooms, scallions, and bean sprouts to the wok and stir-fry for about 5 minutes.

3. Add the noodles to the wok, toss well, and stir-fry for an additional 5 minutes. Drizzle the soy sauce and sesame oil over the noodles and toss until thoroughly combined. Transfer to warm bowls and serve immediately.

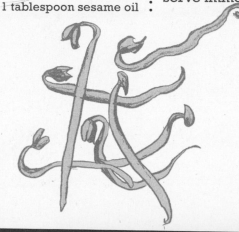

WOK ON!
(HOW TO COOK, SERVE & EAT NOODLES)

It's worth noting that wheat-based noodles differ from pasta in that they are made with a softer variety of wheat. The durum wheat used in pasta creates a firmer end product than silky noodles with their characteristic soft texture, which also cook more quickly than pasta.

Naturally, the type of noodle you choose determines how you cook and eat it. It's always best to refer to the cooking directions given on the product's packaging—cooking time may also differ according to the manufacturer.

Noodle dough tends to have plenty of salt already added to help develop the softer protein and bind the dough. This helps to preserve the noodles once dried. Therefore there is no need to add salt to the cooking water. The other main difference is that pasta is extruded (like squeezing toothpaste from a tube) whereas noodle dough is rolled and then cut.

Soaking vs. Boiling

To rehydrate dried noodles, either soak them in boiling water off the heat, then drain and cook, or add them to a large saucepan filled with boiling water or flavored broth.

When cooking noodles in advance, such as before adding to a stir-fry, the noodles can be cooked and drained, then placed in a bowl of ice-cold water to stop the cooking process.

water to stop the cooking process. Once cool, drain well and toss in a little toasted sesame oil until needed.

To check whether the noodles are cooked, remove a piece of noodle from the pan, cool momentarily, and then taste to make sure that it's tender. It's hard to undercook noodles, but easy to overcook them, so keep that in mind if you will be adding cooked noodles to a stir-fry.

When adding to a wok or saucepan, first heat the wok or pan to a high temperature, then add the oil. Always lift and toss the noodles instead of trying to stir them in the pan. This helps retain the texture.

Serving Noodles

Noodles are served in a huge number of ways, generally in a hot broth with a dipping sauce or stir-fried with vegetables, meat, or fish, or cold in a salad with a dressing.

The etiquette of eating noodles depends on the country in which you are eating. In China, it's not acceptable to bite off noodles when eating but a slurping action is the norm. The chopsticks are used to help the noodles into the mouth.

TERIYAKI CHICKEN

SERVES: 4

PREP TIME: 10 MINS, PLUS MARINATING

COOK TIME: 25 MINS

INGREDIENTS

4 boneless chicken breasts (about 6 ounces each), with or without skin

¼ cup teriyaki sauce, plus extra if needed

peanut or corn oil, for brushing

SESAME NOODLES

8 ounces dried thin soba noodles

1 tablespoon toasted sesame oil

2 tablespoons sesame seeds, toasted

2 tablespoons finely chopped fresh parsley

salt and pepper, to taste

1. Using a sharp knife, score each chicken breast diagonally across three times. Rub all over with teriyaki sauce. Set aside in the refrigerator to marinate for at least 10 minutes and up to 24 hours.

2. Meanwhile, preheat the broiler to high. To make the sesame noodles, cook the noodles according to the package directions. Drain well and set aside.

3. Lightly brush a ridged grill pan with peanut oil. Add the chicken breasts, skin-side up, and brush again with a little extra teriyaki sauce.

4. Grill the chicken breasts, brushing occasionally with extra teriyaki sauce, for 15 minutes, or until tender and no longer pink when cut into the thickest part of the meat.

5. Meanwhile, heat a wok over high heat. Add the sesame oil and heat until it shimmers.

6. Add the noodles and stir around to heat through, then stir in the sesame seeds and parsley. Season with salt and pepper.

7. Transfer the chicken breasts to warm plates and serve immediately with the noodles.

UDON NOODLES WITH HOISIN TURKEY SAUCE

SERVES: 4   **PREP TIME: 10 MINS**   **COOK TIME: 15 MINS**

INGREDIENTS

1 pound fresh udon noodles

2 tablespoons vegetable oil

2 tablespoons finely chopped fresh ginger

2 garlic cloves, finely chopped

1–2 red jalapeño chiles, seeded and finely chopped

1¼ pounds fresh ground turkey

2 cups green beans (1-inch pieces)

½ cup diced water chestnuts

1 tablespoon Chinese rice wine, dry sherry, or dry white wine

3 scallions, white and pale green parts thinly sliced, to garnish

SAUCE

½ cup hoisin sauce

¼ cup chicken stock or water

2 tablespoons sesame oil

2 tablespoons rice vinegar

1. Cook the noodles according to the package directions. Drain and keep warm.

2. Heat 1 tablespoon of the oil in a large skillet over medium–high heat. Add the ginger and cook, stirring, for 1 minute. Add the garlic and chiles and cook, stirring, for an additional minute. Add the turkey and cook, stirring and breaking up the meat with a spatula, until the meat is brown all over. Transfer the meat to a bowl.

3. To make the sauce, stir together all of the ingredients in a small bowl and set aside.

4. Heat the remaining oil in a saucepan. Add the beans and water chestnuts and cook, stirring frequently, for 4 minutes, or until the beans begin to soften. Add the wine and cook, stirring and scraping up any sediment from the bottom of the pan, for about 1 minute, until the liquid has almost evaporated. Add the reserved turkey to the pan with the hoisin sauce mixture. Cook, stirring occasionally, for an additional 4 minutes, or until the sauce is thickened and the beans are tender.

5. Toss the turkey mixture with the noodles, garnish with the scallions, and serve immediately.

THAI GREEN CHICKEN CURRY & UDON NOODLES

SERVES: 4 **PREP TIME: 10 MINS** **COOK TIME: 15 MINS**

INGREDIENTS

1 tablespoon vegetable oil

1 shallot, diced

1–3 teaspoons Thai green curry paste

1¾ cups coconut milk

1 tablespoon Thai fish sauce

juice of 1 lime

1 tablespoon packed light brown sugar

½ cup fresh basil leaves

½ cup fresh cilantro leaves

1 pound fresh udon noodles

2½ cups shredded, cooked chicken

3 scallions, thinly sliced, to garnish

1. Heat the oil in a nonstick skillet over medium heat. Add the shallot and cook for 5 minutes, until soft. Add the curry paste and cook, stirring, for 1 minute.

2. Scoop off the thick cream that will have risen to the top of the coconut milk. Add the cream to the pan with the fish sauce, lime juice, and sugar. Cook, stirring frequently, for 1–2 minutes. Stir in the remaining coconut milk and bring the mixture to a boil. Reduce the heat to low and simmer, stirring occasionally, for an additional 5 minutes, or until the sauce thickens. Remove from the heat and let cool slightly.

3. Transfer the mixture to a food processor, add the basil and cilantro, and process until smooth and bright green. Return the sauce to the pan and reheat over medium–low heat.

4. Cook the noodles according to the package directions and place them in a large serving bowl.

5. Add the chicken and sauce to the noodles and toss to combine. Serve immediately, garnished with the scallions.

TURKEY MEATBALLS WITH GINGER-SOBA NOODLES

SERVES: 4   **PREP TIME: 15 MINS**   **COOK TIME: 20 MINS**

INGREDIENTS

cooking spray, for greasing
1 pound fresh ground turkey
1 egg, lightly beaten
4 scallions, finely chopped
3 garlic cloves
½ cup finely chopped fresh cilantro
½ cup finely diced water chestnuts
2 tablespoons soy sauce
1 tablespoon sesame oil
½ teaspoon salt
1 cup panko bread crumbs
8 ounces dried soba noodles

SAUCE

4 scallions, finely chopped
½ cup minced fresh ginger
¾ teaspoon salt
¼ cup peanut oil

1. Preheat the oven to 400°F. Line a baking sheet with a sheet of parchment paper and spray it with cooking spray.

2. Combine the turkey, egg, scallions, garlic, cilantro, water chestnuts, soy sauce, sesame oil, salt, and bread crumbs in a medium bowl. Mix well with a fork or your hands, but do not overwork the mixture. Shape the mixture into 1½-inch balls and place them on the prepared baking sheet, spaced well apart. Continue until all of the meat mixture has been shaped into balls. Lightly spray the tops of the meatballs with cooking spray and bake in the preheated oven for 20 minutes, or until cooked through and beginning to brown.

3. Meanwhile, cook the noodles according to the package directions. Place in a large serving bowl.

4. To make the sauce, combine the scallions, ginger, and salt in a medium-sized heatproof bowl. Heat the oil in a small saucepan over high heat until just beginning to smoke. Carefully pour the hot oil over the scallion mixture and stir with a fork.

5. Add the cooked meatballs to the noodles in the bowl, then add the sauce and toss to coat well. Serve immediately.

CHICKEN WITH UDON NOODLES & PEANUTS

SERVES: 4   **PREP TIME: 10 MINS**   **COOK TIME: 5 MINS**

INGREDIENTS

12 ounces fresh udon noodles

1 garlic clove, finely chopped

⅔ cup smooth peanut butter

3 tablespoons low-sodium soy sauce

3 tablespoons unseasoned rice vinegar

2 tablespoons packed light brown sugar

2 teaspoons toasted sesame oil

1 teaspoon chili paste or ¼ teaspoon cayenne pepper

2–3 tablespoons water (optional)

2½ cups shredded cooked chicken

1 cucumber, peeled, seeded, and cut into matchsticks

1 red bell pepper, seeded and cut into matchsticks

3 tablespoons finely chopped fresh cilantro, to garnish

1. Cook the noodles according to the package directions.

2. Meanwhile, put the garlic into a food processor with the peanut butter, soy sauce, vinegar, sugar, oil, and chili paste and process until smooth and well combined. Add the water, a little at a time, until the desired consistency is reached.

3. Drain the noodles and place them in a large bowl. Add the sauce and toss until well coated. Add the chicken, cucumber, and red bell pepper and toss again to combine. Serve immediately, garnished with cilantro.

HERO TIPS For the best flavor, use all-natural peanut butter that is made from nothing but peanuts or peanuts and salt.

SESAME SOBA NOODLES WITH BROILED CHICKEN

SERVES: 4   **PREP TIME: 25 MINS**   **COOK TIME: 20 MINS**

INGREDIENTS

zest and juice of 1 large orange

1 tablespoon packed dark brown sugar

1 tablespoon rice vinegar

1 tablespoon soy sauce

1 garlic clove, finely chopped

1 tablespoon finely chopped fresh ginger

1 pound boneless, skinless chicken breasts, cut into strips

12 ounces dried soba noodles

2 cups sugar snap peas (halved widthwise)

6 small radishes, thinly sliced

4 scallions, thinly sliced, to garnish

SESAME SAUCE

1 garlic clove, peeled

1-inch piece fresh ginger, peeled

⅓ cup tahini

2 tablespoons packed dark brown sugar

2 tablespoons soy sauce

2 tablespoons sesame oil

1 tablespoon rice vinegar

¼ –½ teaspoon hot chili oil

1–2 tablespoons lukewarm water

1. Combine the orange zest and juice, sugar, vinegar, soy sauce, garlic, and ginger in a medium bowl. Add the chicken and toss to coat. Marinate for at least 30 minutes or overnight.

2. Cook the noodles according to the package directions. Drain and keep warm.

3. Preheat the broiler to high. Remove the chicken strips from the marinade (discarding the marinade), and cook under the broiler for about 4 minutes on each side, until cooked through.

4. To make the sesame sauce, process the garlic and ginger in a blender or food processor until finely chopped. Add the tahini, sugar, soy sauce, sesame oil, vinegar, and chili oil and process until smooth. Add the water, a little at a time, until the desired consistency is achieved.

5. Pour the sauce over the warm noodles and toss to coat. Add the sugar snap peas and radishes and toss to combine. Serve the noodles topped with the strips of chicken and garnished with the scallions.

TURKEY WITH CILANTRO PESTO & SOBA NOODLES

SERVES: 6-8

PREP TIME: 10 MINS, PLUS MARINATING

COOK TIME: 20 MINS

INGREDIENTS

¼ cup low-sodium soy sauce

2 teaspoons chili paste

3 garlic cloves, sliced

1 skinless, boneless turkey breast (about 3–4 pounds)

1 pound dried soba noodles

PESTO

2 cups chopped fresh cilantro

½ cup vegetable oil

¼ cup sugar

4 garlic cloves

2 tablespoons finely chopped fresh ginger

2 teaspoons chili paste

juice of 1 lime

2 teaspoons salt

1. Combine the soy sauce, chili paste, and garlic in a bowl large enough to hold the turkey breast. Add the turkey breast and turn to coat. Cover and marinate in the refrigerator for at least 2 hours or overnight.

2. To cook the turkey, let it come to room temperature and preheat the broiler to high. Broil for about 10 minutes on each side, until a meat thermometer inserted into the thickest part registers 165°F.

3. Meanwhile, cook the noodles according to the package directions. Drain and set aside.

4. To make the pesto, combine the cilantro, oil, sugar, garlic, ginger, chili paste, lime juice, and salt in a food processor and process until well combined.

5. Remove the cooked turkey from the broiler, loosely cover with aluminum foil, and let rest for at least 5 minutes before slicing.

6. Toss the noodles with the pesto and slice the turkey into ¼-inch slices. Serve immediately with the noodles.

FROM THE FARM

PORK RAMEN SOUP

SERVES: 4

PREP TIME: 10 MINS, PLUS MARINATING

COOK TIME: 1 HR

INGREDIENTS

1 tablespoon finely chopped fresh ginger

2 tablespoons honey

2 tablespoons soy sauce

2 tablespoons mirin

1 teaspoon sesame oil

1 teaspoon Chinese five spice

1 pork tenderloin (about 1½ pounds)

bean sprouts, pea shoots, and hard-boiled eggs, to garnish

SOUP

1 tablespoon vegetable oil

1 yellow onion, diced

3 garlic cloves, finely chopped

1 tablespoon grated fresh ginger

6⅓ cups chicken stock

8 ounces fresh shiitake mushrooms, stems removed and caps thinly sliced

½ teaspoon rock salt

4 teaspoons low-sodium soy sauce

1 tablespoon Chinese rice wine

1 teaspoon sesame oil

1 pound dried ramen noodles (flavoring envelope discarded, if included)

4 teaspoons miso paste

1. To prepare the pork, stir together the ginger, honey, soy sauce, mirin, sesame oil, and five spice in a large bowl. Add the pork and turn to coat. Cover and refrigerate for at least 2 hours or overnight.

2. To make the soup, heat the vegetable oil in a large saucepan over medium–high heat. Add the onion, garlic, and ginger and cook, stirring, for 5 minutes, or until the onions are translucent and soft. Add the stock, mushrooms, salt, soy sauce, wine, and sesame oil and bring to a boil. Reduce the heat to low and simmer, uncovered, for about 30 minutes.

3. Meanwhile, preheat the oven to 375°F. Place the pork on a baking pan and roast in the preheated oven for 20 minutes.

4. Meanwhile, preheat the grill to high. Transfer the pork to the grill rack and cook for about 5 minutes on each side, until brown and beginning to show grill marks. Reduce the heat to medium–low and continue to cook until a meat thermometer inserted into the thickest part of the meat registers a temperature of 145–155°F. Remove from the grill, loosely cover with aluminum foil, and let rest for 5 minutes before slicing.

5. Bring the soup back to a boil and add the noodles, breaking them up to be sure they are all submerged in the liquid. Cook for about 3 minutes, until the noodles are tender. Stir in the miso paste until fully dissolved.

6. Thinly slice the pork. Ladle the soup into bowls, top with several slices of pork, garnish with the bean sprouts, pea shoots, and hard-boiled eggs, and serve immediately.

RAMEN MEATBALL SOUP

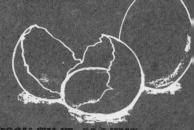

SERVES: 4   **PREP TIME: 15 MINS**   **COOK TIME: 50 MINS**

INGREDIENTS
MEATBALLS

cooking spray, for greasing

1 pound fresh ground round or ground sirloin

1 cup panko bread crumbs

1 egg, lightly beaten

1 tablespoon finely chopped fresh ginger

2 garlic cloves, finely chopped

3 scallions, finely chopped

1 teaspoon salt

1 teaspoon sesame oil

SOUP

1 tablespoon vegetable oil

2 garlic cloves, finely chopped

1 tablespoon grated fresh ginger

6½ cups beef stock

¼ cup soy sauce

1 tablespoon sake or dry white wine

1 teaspoon salt

1 teaspoon sesame oil

1 pound dried ramen noodles (flavoring envelope discarded, if included)

4 scallions, thinly sliced, to garnish

1. Preheat the oven to 400°F. Line a large baking pan with a sheet of parchment paper and lightly spray it with cooking spray.

2. To make the meatballs, combine the beef, bread crumbs, egg, ginger, garlic, scallions, salt, and oil in a large bowl and mix well. Shape the mixture into 1-inch balls, placing them on the prepared baking sheet as you work. Bake in the preheated oven for 12–14 minutes, until lightly browned and cooked through.

3. To make the soup, heat the vegetable oil in a large saucepan over medium–high heat. Add the garlic and ginger and cook, stirring, for about 3 minutes, until soft. Add the stock, soy sauce, sake, salt, and sesame oil and bring to a boil. Reduce the heat to low and simmer, uncovered, for about 30 minutes. Add the meatballs.

4. Bring the soup back to a boil and add the noodles, breaking them up to be sure they are all submerged in the liquid. Cook for about 3 minutes, until the noodles are soft. Serve hot, garnished with scallions.

STEAK & SOBA NOODLE SALAD

SERVES: 4

PREP TIME: 15 MINS, PLUS MARINATING

COOK TIME: 10 MINS

INGREDIENTS

2 tablespoons soy sauce

1 tablespoon Chinese rice wine, dry sherry, or dry white wine

2 garlic cloves, finely chopped

2 teaspoons packed light brown sugar

2 tablespoons olive oil

1 tenderloin steak (about 1 pound)

⅓ cup toasted sesame seeds, to garnish

DRESSING

juice of 1 lime

2 tablespoons white miso paste

1 tablespoon low-sodium soy sauce

1 tablespoon unseasoned rice vinegar

¼ cup vegetable oil

1 tablespoon sesame oil

SALAD

12 ounces dried soba noodles

½ large cucumber

3½ cups arugula

¼ cup chopped fresh cilantro

3 scallions, thinly sliced

1. Combine the soy sauce, wine, garlic, sugar, and olive oil in a large bowl. Add the steak and turn to coat. Refrigerate for at least 2 hours or overnight.

2. To cook the steak, preheat the broiler to high. Remove the steak from the marinade (discarding the marinade), place under the broiler, and cook for 4–5 minutes on each side for medium-rare, or a few minutes longer if you prefer your steak more well done. Remove from the broiler, loosely cover with aluminum foil, and let rest for at least 5 minutes. Slice the steak into ¼-inch-thick slices.

3. Meanwhile, prepare the dressing. Combine the lime juice, miso paste, soy sauce, and rice vinegar in a small bowl and whisk to combine. Add the vegetable oil and sesame oil and whisk until the dressing is emulsified.

4. To make the salad, cook the noodles according to the package directions, drain, and cool. Peel the cucumber and cut in half lengthwise, seed, and finely slice. Place in a bowl with the remaining salad ingredients, add some dressing, and toss to combine and coat.

5. To serve, divide the salad among individual serving plates and top each with several slices of steak. Drizzle a little dressing over the steak and garnish with the sesame seeds.

SICHUAN NUMBING BEEF SALAD

SERVES: 4

PREP TIME: 10 MINS, PLUS MARINATING

COOK TIME: 10 MINS

INGREDIENTS

12 ounces tenderloin steak

4 ounces egg noodles

1 small red onion, halved and thinly sliced into crescents

6 radishes, sliced

4 good handfuls of peppery leaves such as tatsoi, mustard greens, and arugula

1½ tablespoons peanut oil

1 teaspoon Sichuan pepper, crushed

MARINADE

4 teaspoons Chinese rice wine or dry sherry

1½ teaspoons soy sauce

4 teaspoons sugar

2 tablespoons hoisin sauce

1-inch piece fresh ginger, squeezed in a garlic press

DRESSING

2 teaspoons Sichuan pepper, crushed

1½ tablespoons light soy sauce

1½ tablespoons rice vinegar

2 tablespoons cold-pressed sesame oil

1. Trim any fat from the steak. Slice the meat into thin strips and put in a shallow dish. Combine the marinade ingredients and pour over the beef. Let marinate for 30 minutes.

2. Cook the noodles according to the package directions. Drain, let cool, and snip into shorter lengths. Whisk the dressing ingredients until well blended. Combine the noodles, onion, radishes, and salad greens in a large bowl. Whisk the dressing again and pour two-thirds of it over the salad. Toss to distribute the noodles, then divide among individual serving plates.

3. Heat a wok over medium–high heat, then add the peanut oil and Sichuan pepper. Stir for a few seconds to flavor the oil. Add the beef and marinade, and stir-fry for 4–5 minutes, until caramelized. Remove with a slotted spoon and pile on top of the salad. Pour over the remaining dressing. Serve immediately.

KNOW YOUR NOODLES!
(DIFFERENT TYPES OF NOODLES)

Noodles are generally sold in three basic formats: precooked (sold both chilled and at room temperature), dried, and fresh.

Of course, the choice you make depends on where you might be shopping and how much time you have available. The dried and long-life precooked noodles are the most convenient to use.

With regards to the different types of noodles available, there are many varieties, but we will concentrate on the following:

Soba
Ramen
Udon
Rice
Egg

SOBA

In general, soba are made with buckwheat flour (although they can also be bought made with rice flour). Unlike its name suggests, buckwheat contains no gluten or wheat. Soba noodles can contain 40–100 percent buckwheat, with the rest of the flour used being wheat. It's the buckwheat that gives the noodles their distinctive color and nuttiness. Soba are the most popular noodles in Japan, and they come in a variety of thicknesses.

RAMEN

In Japan, ramen is seen as comfort food and is especially popular. Whether its origins are from China or Japan is unknown, but there are many regional specialties, and restaurants devoted to ramen-based meals cooked by chefs who specialize in the cooking techniques associated with ramen.

Ramen generally relates to a broth-base dish in which chukamen noodles are served, made with wheat flour. There are other uses for ramen noodles: for example, the ramen burger. This uses cooked noodles, pressed into patty shapes, and then fried in place of a bread roll for a completely new burger eating experience!

UDON

In general thick and white, these noodles are made with a semi-whole-wheat flour. They are light and easily digested and the slow drying time helps give them a good flavor. They are sold in different thicknesses, and they work best in soups and broths but can also be used just as any other noodle.

RICE

Made from rice flour and water, these wiry, thin noodles are common in Southeast Asia and southern China. They are sold in a variety of thicknesses and are also available made with brown rice flour. The same dough is used to make rice wrappers. They are perfect for use in stir-fries, soups, and salads.

EGG

Made with wheat flour, water, and eggs (can be duck eggs). They vary in width and color, from a pale cream to deep yellow, depending on the amount of egg content. In general, they cook fast and are a good all-purpose noodle.

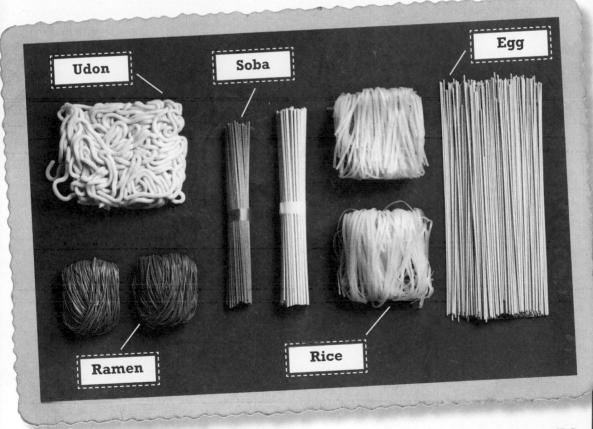

Udon

Soba

Egg

Ramen

Rice

RAMEN BURGER

SERVES: 2

PREP TIME: 10 MINS. PLUS CHILLING

COOK TIME: 15 MINS

INGREDIENTS
NOODLE BUN

6 ounces ramen noodles (flavoring envelope discarded, if included), cooked according to the package directions, rinsed, drained, and left to dry

2 eggs, lightly beaten

2 scallions, thinly sliced

2 tablespoons vegetable oil

BURGER

8 ounces ground chuck beef

1 teaspoon grated fresh ginger

2 scallions, thinly sliced

1 tablespoon hoisin sauce

2 teaspoons sriracha sauce

1 teaspoon low-sodium soy sauce

1½ teaspoons sesame oil

TO SERVE

½ cup shredded cabbage

2 tablespoons finely chopped fresh cilantro

hoisin sauce, sriracha, or ketchup (optional)

1. Combine the noodles, eggs, and scallions in a bowl and stir to mix. Place an equal amount of the noodle mixture in each of four flat bowls with a diameter of 4–5 inches. Place plastic wrap over the surface of the bowls and place a heavy glass or can in the bowls to weigh down the noodles. Chill in the refrigerator for about 30 minutes.

2. Meanwhile, to make the patties, preheat the broiler to medium. Combine the beef with the ginger, scallions, hoisin sauce, sriracha sauce, soy sauce, and sesame oil in a bowl and mix well. Shape the mixture into two patties.

3. Place the patties under the preheated broiler and cook for 4–5 minutes on each side, or until cooked to your preference.

4. To cook the buns, heat the oil in a large nonstick skillet over medium–high heat. Remove the chilled noodle buns from the bowls, place in the pan, and cook on each side for 5 minutes, or until brown and crisp.

5. To serve, place each patty on one of the noodle buns. Top with cabbage, cilantro, and hoisin sauce, if using. Add the bun lid and serve.

PORK & NOODLES IN PLUM SAUCE

With its tangy sweet-sour flavor, plum sauce is a great combination with pork.

MAKES: 4   **PREP TIME: 10 MINS**   **COOK TIME: 10-12 MINS**

INGREDIENTS

1¼ pounds pork tenderloin
2 tablespoons peanut oil
1 orange bell pepper, seeded and sliced
1 bunch scallions, sliced
8 ounces oyster mushrooms, sliced
3 cups fresh bean sprouts
2 tablespoons dry sherry
⅔ cup plum sauce
8 ounces medium egg noodles
salt and pepper, to taste
chopped fresh cilantro, to garnish

1. Slice the pork into long, thin strips. Heat a wok over medium–high heat, then add the oil. Add the pork strips and stir-fry for 2–3 minutes, until cooked through.

2. Add the orange bell pepper and stir-fry for 2 minutes, then add the scallions, mushrooms, and bean sprouts.

3. Stir-fry for 2–3 minutes, then add the sherry and plum sauce and heat until boiling. Season well with salt and pepper.

4. Meanwhile, cook the noodles according to the package directions. Drain, then add to the wok and toss well. Serve immediately, garnished with the fresh cilantro.

HERO TIPS

For a spicier version of this dish, simply add 2 tablespoons of chili sauce along with the sherry and plum sauce.

MINTY LAMB MEATBALLS WITH SOBA NOODLES

SERVES: 4   **PREP TIME: 25 MINS**   **COOK TIME: 15 MINS**

INGREDIENTS
MEATBALLS

cooking spray, for greasing

1 pound fresh ground lamb

1 shallot, finely chopped

2 garlic cloves, finely chopped

1 tablespoon each, finely chopped fresh mint leaves and cilantro leaves

2 serrano chiles, seeded and chopped

1 tablespoon Thai fish sauce

1 cup panko bread crumbs

1 egg

12 ounces dried soba noodles

¼ cup crushed dry-roasted peanuts, to garnish

PESTO

2 serrano chiles

1-inch piece fresh ginger

4 garlic cloves

1 cup fresh mint leaves

¼ cup fresh basil leaves

juice of 1 lime

1 tablespoon Thai fish sauce

1 tablespoon sugar

3 tablespoons vegetable oil

1. Preheat the oven to 400°F. Line a large baking pan with a sheet of parchment paper and spray it with the cooking spray.

2. To make the meatballs, combine the lamb, shallot, garlic, mint, cilantro, chiles, fish sauce, bread crumbs, and egg and mix well. Shape the meat mixture into 1½-inch balls and place them on the prepared pan. Lightly spray the tops with the cooking spray and bake in the preheated oven for 15 minutes, or until cooked through.

3. Meanwhile, to make the pesto, halve and seed the chiles and peel and chop the ginger. Put into a food processor with the garlic and process until finely chopped. Add the mint, basil, lime juice, fish sauce, sugar, and oil and process to a smooth puree.

4. Cook the noodles according to the package directions. Drain and toss the noodles with the pesto in a large bowl. Serve immediately topped with the meatballs and garnished with peanuts.

SESAME UDON NOODLES WITH STIR-FRIED BEEF

SERVES: 4

PREP TIME: 15 MINS, PLUS MARINATING

COOK TIME: 10 MINS

INGREDIENTS

1 tablespoon sugar

1 tablespoon soy sauce

1 tablespoon sesame oil

1 pound tenderloin steak, thinly sliced

1 pound fresh udon noodles

2 tablespoons vegetable oil

2 tablespoons toasted sesame seeds and 3 thinly sliced scallions, to garnish

SESAME SAUCE

1 garlic clove, peeled

1-inch piece fresh ginger, peeled

¼ cup tahini

2 tablespoons packed dark brown sugar

2 tablespoons soy sauce

2 tablespoons sesame oil

1 tablespoon rice vinegar

¼–½ teaspoon hot chili oil

1–2 tablespoons lukewarm water

1. Combine the sugar, soy sauce, and sesame oil in a medium bowl. Add the beef, stir to coat, and let marinate for about 30 minutes.

2. Meanwhile, to make the sesame sauce, put the garlic and ginger into a blender or food processor and process until finely chopped. Add the tahini, sugar, soy sauce, sesame oil, vinegar, and chili oil and process until smooth. Add the water, a little at a time, until the desired consistency is achieved.

3. Cook the noodles according to the package directions, drain, and keep warm.

4. Heat the vegetable oil in a large skillet over medium–high heat. Remove the beef from the marinade (discarding the marinade) and add it to the hot pan. Stir-fry, stirring frequently, for about 4 minutes, until brown and cooked through.

5. In a large bowl, toss the noodles with some of the sauce until well coated. Divide the noodles among four serving plates and top with some of the beef. Drizzle a little more sesame sauce over the beef and serve, garnished with sesame seeds and scallions.

DAN DAN NOODLES WITH PORK

SERVES: 4   **PREP TIME: 5 MINS**   **COOK TIME: 15 MINS**

INGREDIENTS

1 pound fresh udon noodles
1 tablespoon vegetable oil
12 ounces fresh ground pork
½ teaspoon salt
¼ teaspoon pepper
2 tablespoons finely chopped fresh ginger
¾ cup chicken stock
¼ cup tahini
2 tablespoons rice vinegar
2 tablespoons soy sauce
2 tablespoons packed light brown sugar
2–3 teaspoons chili oil
1 teaspoon sesame oil
1 teaspoon crushed Sichuan peppercorns
2 tablespoons chopped roasted peanuts and
3 scallions, thinly sliced, to garnish

1. Cook the noodles according to the package directions. Drain and set aside.

2. Heat the oil in a large skillet over medium–high heat. Add the pork, salt, and pepper and cook, stirring and breaking the meat up with a spatula, until brown all over.

3. Add the ginger and cook, stirring, for an additional 1–2 minutes, until fragrant. Add the stock, tahini, vinegar, soy sauce, sugar, chili oil, sesame oil, and peppercorns and bring to a boil, stirring to mix well. Simmer for 5 minutes, or until the sauce thickens.

4. Toss the noodles and sauce together in a large bowl. Serve immediately, garnished with peanuts and scallions.

HERO TIPS

If you cannot find tahini, or simply don't like it, you can substitute smooth peanut butter instead.

CHOW FUN NOODLES WITH BEEF STRIPS

Chow fun rice noodles are popular in both Vietnam and Thailand.

SERVES: 4 **PREP TIME: 10 MINS, PLUS STANDING** **COOK TIME: 5-10 MINS**

INGREDIENTS

12 ounces tenderloin or sirloin

2 tablespoons soy sauce

2 tablespoons toasted sesame oil

8 ounces flat rice noodles

2 tablespoons peanut oil

1 onion, sliced into thin wedges

2 garlic cloves, crushed

1-inch piece fresh ginger, chopped

1 red chile, thinly sliced

8 ounces baby broccoli

½ head Chinese greens, sliced

chili oil, to serve

1. Slice the beef into thin strips, place in a bowl, and sprinkle with the soy sauce and toasted sesame oil. Cover and let stand for 15 minutes.

2. Prepare the noodles according to the package directions. Drain and set aside.

3. Heat a wok over high heat, then add 1 tablespoon of peanut oil. Add the beef and stir-fry until evenly browned. Remove and keep to one side.

4. Add the remaining oil and stir-fry the onion, garlic, ginger, and chile for 1 minute.

5. Add the broccoli and stir-fry for 2 minutes, then add the greens and stir-fry for 1 minute. Serve the noodles, beef, and vegetables immediately, drizzled with chili oil.

PORK PAD THAI

SERVES: 4   **PREP TIME: 10 MINS**   **COOK TIME: 6-10 MINS**

INGREDIENTS

8 ounces thick dried rice noodles

2 tablespoons peanut oil or vegetable oil

4 scallions, coarsely chopped

2 garlic cloves, crushed

2 red chiles, seeded and sliced

8 ounces pork tenderloin, trimmed and thinly sliced

4 ounces cooked, peeled large shrimp

juice of 1 lime

2 tablespoons Thai fish sauce

2 eggs, beaten

½ cup fresh bean sprouts

handful of chopped fresh cilantro

⅓ cup unsalted peanuts, chopped

lime wedges, to serve

1. Prepare the noodles according to the package directions. Drain and set aside.

2. Heat a wok over medium–high heat, then add the oil. Add the scallions, garlic and chiles and stir-fry for 1–2 minutes. Add the pork and stir-fry over high heat for 1–2 minutes, until cooked through.

3. Add the shrimp, lime juice, fish sauce, and eggs and stir-fry over medium heat for 2–3 minutes, until the eggs are set and the shrimp are heated through.

4. Add the bean sprouts, most of the cilantro, the peanuts, and the noodles and stir-fry for 30 seconds, until heated through. Garnish with the remaining cilantro and serve immediately with lime wedges.

HERO TIPS

This traditional Thai dish has many variations but should always include noodles and peanuts. It is important to use thick rice noodles, which are available in larger supermarkets or online.

LAMB & SQUASH CURRY WITH UDON NOODLES

Udon noodles are perfect for soaking up this rich, spicy sauce. Full-flavored lamb makes this dish especially satisfying, but you can also substitute beef, pork, or chicken.

SERVES: 4 **PREP TIME: 10 MINS** **COOK TIME: 30 MINS**

INGREDIENTS

2 tablespoons vegetable oil

2 shallots, thinly sliced

1 pound lamb shoulder, cut into 1-inch cubes

1–2 tablespoons red Thai curry paste

1¾ cups coconut milk

1 cup vegetable, beef, or chicken stock or water

3 tablespoons Thai fish sauce

2 tablespoons packed light brown sugar

3 lemongrass stalks, cut into 3-inch pieces and bruised with the side of a heavy knife

3 kaffir lime leaves, julienned

½ butternut squash, peeled and cut into 1-inch cubes

12 ounces dried udon noodles

juice of 1 lime

¼ cup chopped fresh cilantro, to garnish

1. Heat the oil in a large, deep skillet over medium-high heat. Add the shallots and cook, stirring frequently, for 5 minutes, or until soft. Add the lamb and cook, stirring frequently, until brown all over.

2. Stir in the curry paste and about 2 tablespoons of the thick cream from the top of the container of coconut milk. Cook for 1 minute. Add the remaining coconut milk, the stock, fish sauce, sugar, lemongrass, and lime leaves. Bring to a boil and add the squash. Reduce the heat to medium–low, cover, and simmer for 15–20 minutes, until the pumpkin is tender.

3. Meanwhile, cook the noodles according to the package directions. Drain and set aside.

4. When the squash is tender, add the drained noodles to the skillet and cook for 2–3 minutes, until heated through. Stir in the lime juice and serve immediately, garnished with cilantro.

FROM THE SEA

SALMON RAMEN

SERVES: 4   **PREP TIME: 10-15 MINS**   **COOK TIME: 10-15 MINS**

INGREDIENTS

4¼ cups fish stock or vegetable stock

1 large garlic clove

½ teaspoon light soy sauce

4 salmon fillets (about 5 ounces each), skinned

peanut or sunflower oil, for brushing

4 ounces dried ramen or fine egg noodles

3½ cups baby spinach leaves

4 scallions, chopped

TERIYAKI GLAZE

2½ tablespoons sake

2½ tablespoons dark soy sauce

2 tablespoons mirin or sweet sherry

1½ teaspoons packed light brown sugar

½ garlic clove, minced

¼-inch-piece fresh ginger, minced

TO SERVE

1 cup fresh bean sprouts

1 fresh green chile, seeded and sliced

fresh cilantro leaves

1. Preheat the broiler to high. Put the stock in a saucepan, add the garlic clove and soy sauce, and bring to a boil.

2. Mix together the ingredients for the teriyaki glaze and brush one surface of each salmon fillet with the glaze. Lightly brush the broiler rack with oil and cook the salmon under the preheated broiler for 4 minutes on only one side. The flesh should flake easily and the center should remain a bright pink. Remove the fish from the broiler and set aside.

3. Cook the noodles according to the package directions. Drain and set aside.

4. Remove the garlic from the stock, then bring the stock back to a boil. Drop in the spinach leaves and scallions and cook until the leaves are just wilted. Use a slotted spoon to remove the spinach and scallions from the pan and divide them among warm bowls. Divide the noodles among the bowls, then add a salmon fillet to each. Carefully pour the boiling stock into each bowl.

5. Sprinkle with the bean sprouts, chile slices, and cilantro leaves and serve immediately.

SPICY UDON NOODLES & SHRIMP

SERVES: 4

PREP TIME: 15 MINS, PLUS MARINATING

COOK TIME: 35 MINS

INGREDIENTS

2 tablespoons vegetable oil

2 leeks, halved lengthwise and thinly sliced

2 garlic cloves, finely chopped

2 lemongrass stalks, pounded with the side of a heavy knife and cut into 2-inch lengths

2 hot red chiles, sliced into rings

1 teaspoon salt

6⅓ cups vegetable stock

grated zest and juice of 1 lime

6 kaffir lime leaves

12 ounces fresh udon noodles

shredded red cabbage and shredded carrot, to garnish

SHRIMP

1 tablespoon finely chopped fresh ginger

2 garlic cloves, finely chopped

½ cup soy sauce

¼ cup lime juice

1 tablespoon sugar

2 tablespoons vegetable oil

1 pound shrimp, peeled and deveined

1. Heat the oil in a large saucepan over medium–high heat. Add the leeks and cook, stirring, for about 5 minutes, until soft. Add the garlic, lemongrass, chiles, and salt and cook for an additional minute. Add the stock, lime zest and juice, and lime leaves and bring to a boil. Reduce the heat and simmer for about 20 minutes. Remove the lemongrass pieces and lime leaves.

2. Meanwhile, soak eight wooden skewers in water until needed. Whisk together the ginger, garlic, soy sauce, lime juice, and sugar in a medium bowl. Add the vegetable oil and whisk to emulsify. Add the shrimp and toss to coat. Let marinate at room temperature for about 15 minutes.

3. Preheat the broiler to high. Remove the shrimp from the marinade and thread them onto the pre-soaked skewers. Place under the broiler and cook for about 2 minutes on each side, until the shrimp are pink and cooked through.

4. Bring the soup back to a low boil, add the noodles, reduce the heat, and simmer for about 5 minutes, until the noodles are tender.

5. Divide the soup among warm bowls, top each portion with shredded carrot and cabbage and two shrimp skewers, and serve immediately.

SOBA NOODLE NIÇOISE SALAD

SERVES: 4   **PREP TIME: 25 MINS**   **COOK TIME: 2 MINS**

INGREDIENTS

1 tablespoon vegetable oil
1 pound sushi grade ahi tuna
¼ cup black sesame seeds
salt and pepper, to taste

DRESSING

¼ cup rice wine vinegar
1 tablespoon soy sauce
2 teaspoons wasabi paste
½ cup vegetable oil

SALAD

12 ounces dried soba noodles,
cooked according to the
package directions
2 cups green beans, blanched
in lightly salted boiling
water until tender but still
firm to the bite
4 hard-boiled eggs, sliced
12 cherry tomatoes, halved
2 ounces thinly sliced
pickled ginger

1. Heat the oil in a large skillet over high heat. Season the tuna on both sides with salt and pepper. Spread the sesame seeds on a plate in a thin layer. Press the pieces of tuna onto the sesame seeds to coat both sides. When the oil begins to shimmer, add the pieces of tuna. Cook for about 1 minute on each side, until the outside of the fish begins to brown and there is just a thin layer of opaqueness at the edge. The center of the tuna should still be pink. Remove from the pan and let rest for several minutes, then cut into ¼-inch-thick slices and chill in the refrigerator while you prepare the rest of the dish.

2. To make the dressing, combine the vinegar, soy sauce, and wasabi paste in a small bowl and whisk to combine. Add the oil and whisk until emulsified.

3. To make the salad, place the noodles in a large bowl and toss with some of the dressing until well coated. In a separate bowl, toss the beans with some of the dressing. Divide the noodles, beans, eggs, tomatoes, ginger, and sliced tuna among serving plates. Drizzle a little dressing over the tuna slices and serve immediately.

UDON NOODLE STIR-FRY WITH FISH CAKE & GINGER

Made with pureed white fish, Japanese fish cake comes prerolled and ready for slicing.

SERVES: 2　　　　**PREP TIME: 10 MINS**　　　　**COOK TIME: 5-10 MINS**

INGREDIENTS

2 (5½-ounce) packages
ready-to-wok udon noodles

1 leek, shredded

2 cups bean sprouts

8 shiitake mushrooms,
finely sliced

2 pieces Japanese fish
cake, sliced

12 shrimp, peeled
and deveined

2 eggs, beaten

1 tablespoon peanut oil
or vegetable oil

2 tablespoons shoyu
(Japanese soy sauce)

3 tablespoons mirin

2 tablespoons chopped fresh
cilantro leaves

TO SERVE

chili oil

2 scallions, finely sliced

2 tablespoons shredded
beni-shoga (red ginger)

1. Rinse the noodles under cold running water to remove any oil and transfer to a bowl.

2. Add the leek, bean sprouts, mushrooms, fish cake, shrimp, and eggs to the noodles and mix well to combine.

3. Heat a wok over high heat. Add a little oil and heat until hot. Add the noodle mixture and stir-fry until golden and the shrimp turn pink and start to curl. Add the shoyu, mirin, and cilantro and toss together.

4. Divide the noodles between two bowls and drizzle with the chili oil. Sprinkle with the scallions and beni-shoga and serve immediately.

STIR-FRIED RICE NOODLES WITH MARINATED FISH

A tangy chile, lime, and fish sauce marinade adds sensational flavor to this impressive dish.

MAKES: 4

PREP TIME: 10 MINS, PLUS MARINATING

COOK TIME: 5 MINS

INGREDIENTS

1 pound monkfish or cod, cubed

8 ounces salmon fillets, cubed

4 ounces thick rice noodles

2 tablespoons vegetable oil or peanut oil

2 shallots, sliced

2 garlic cloves, finely chopped

1 fresh red chile, seeded and chopped

2 tablespoons Thai soy sauce

2 tablespoons chili sauce

sprigs of fresh cilantro, to garnish

MARINADE

2 tablespoons vegetable oil or peanut oil

2 fresh green chiles, seeded and chopped

grated zest and juice of 1 lime

1 tablespoon Thai fish sauce

1. Combine the marinade ingredients and pour over the fish. Let marinate for 2 hours.

2. Prepare the noodles according to the package directions. Drain and set aside.

3. Heat a wok over medium–high heat and add the oil. Sauté the shallots, garlic, and red chile until lightly browned. Add the soy sauce and chili sauce. Add the fish and the marinade to the wok and stir-fry gently for 2–3 minutes, until cooked through.

4. Add the noodles and stir gently. Garnish with cilantro and serve immediately.

MISO-GLAZED COD WITH SOBA NOODLES

This sweet and salty miso glaze is simple to make, but adds a rich flavor that nicely complements a mild, meaty fish such as cod.

SERVES: 4

PREP TIME: 5 MINS, PLUS MARINATING

COOK TIME: 12 MINS

INGREDIENTS

⅓ cup white miso paste

3 tablespoons packed light brown sugar

2 tablespoons mirin or sake

1–2 tablespoons water, if needed

4 cod fillets (about 5 ounces each)

12 ounces dried soba noodles

1 tablespoon sesame oil

1 tablespoon toasted sesame seeds and 3 scallions, thinly sliced, to garnish

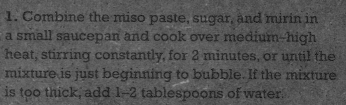

1. Combine the miso paste, sugar, and mirin in a small saucepan and cook over medium-high heat, stirring constantly, for 2 minutes, or until the mixture is just beginning to bubble. If the mixture is too thick, add 1–2 tablespoons of water.

2. Pat the fish fillets dry and place them in a single layer in a baking dish. Brush a little of the miso mixture on each fish fillet and marinate in the refrigerator for 30 minutes.

3. Cook the noodles according to the package directions. Drain and toss with the sesame oil.

4. Preheat the oven to 375°F and preheat the broiler to high. Cook the fish under the broiler for 4 minutes, or until the glaze begins to caramelize. Brush the remaining miso mixture on the fish and bake in the preheated oven for about 5 minutes, until the fish is cooked through and flakes easily with a fork.

5. To serve, divide the noodles among four serving plates. Top each serving with a fish fillet and garnish with sesame seeds and scallions.

UDON IT?
(THE CLASSIC & BEST NOODLE PARTNERS)

Fresh Chiles

The smaller the chile, the hotter it is. Green varieties have more heat than the red because they sweeten as they ripen. To prepare, rinse, halve and remove the seeds (unless the recipe says otherwise). Always wash the utensils before preparing other foods and do not touch your eyes while preparing chiles.

Dried Red Chiles

These are extremely hot so add with caution, or simply use to flavor cooking oil.

Ginger

Essential in so many dishes, this pungent, vibrant, fresh-tasting root adds a distinctive flavor.

Fresh ginger root is the preferred choice. Always choose a root that is plump with smooth skin.

To use, simply peel away the skin and grate or finely chop. Store the prepared ginger in the refrigerator for up to three days or freeze in ice cube trays.

Mirin

A variety of rice wine, and similar to sake but with a lower alcohol content. This sweet Japanese condiment is often used to balance salty sauces, or in dipping sauces.

Miso

Traditional miso paste is a staple Japanese food and seasoning made by fermenting rice barley and or soybeans. This versatile ingredient adds an earthy, salty flavor, giving a good savory base. It can be used as a soup, as the basis for sauces, or spread onto meat or fish.

White miso is fermented for less time and is sweeter and lighter, making it more suitable for salad dressings, marinades, or broths.

Rice Wine

Commonly used as and when you might use wine in cooking: for example, in marinades and sauces. It's made by fermenting glutinous rice, yeast, and spring water.

Rice Vinegar

Vinegars made from rice are widely used in Chinese cooking and there are several varieties: white rice vinegar is mild and light, the black vinegar is fairly mild, and the red version is sweet and spicy.

Soy Sauce

Made from soybeans, flour, and water that has been fermented and aged, the sauce is the result of the distilling.

Light Soy

Although light in color, it has more flavor and a higher salt content, making it better for cooking.

Dark Soy

The longer ageing process gives this sauce its rich, dark color. It's best used as a condiment for finished dishes or as a dipping sauce.

Thai Fish Sauce

A widely used ingredient in Southeast Asian cuisine made by fermenting anchovies in a salt solution. This fish sauce adds a salty note to savory dishes. It is known as nam pla in Thailand and nuoc nam in Vietnam, where it is also widely used.

SPICY SHRIMP WITH GARLIC NOODLES

SERVES: 4   **PREP TIME: 10 MINS**   **COOK TIME: 15 MINS**

INGREDIENTS

8 ounces cooked jumbo shrimp, peeled

¼ cup sweet chili dipping sauce

¼ cup peanut oil or vegetable oil

4 scallions, chopped

2 cups diagonally halved snow peas

1 tablespoon Thai red curry paste

1¾ cups coconut milk

⅓ cup drained and rinsed, canned bamboo shoots

½ cup fresh bean sprouts

4 ounces dried medium egg noodles

2 garlic cloves, crushed

handful of fresh cilantro, chopped

1. Toss the shrimp with the chili sauce in a bowl. Cover and set aside.

2. Heat half the oil in a preheated wok, add the scallions and snow peas, and stir-fry over medium–high heat for 2–3 minutes. Add the curry paste and stir well. Pour in the coconut milk and bring gently to a boil, stirring occasionally. Add the bamboo shoots and bean sprouts and cook, stirring, for 1 minute. Stir in the shrimp and chili sauce, reduce the heat, and simmer for 1–2 minutes, until just heated through.

3. Meanwhile, cook the noodles according to the package directions. Drain and return to the pan.

4. Heat the remaining oil in a small nonstick skillet, add the garlic, and stir-fry over high heat for 30 seconds. Add to the drained noodles with half the cilantro and toss together until well mixed. Transfer the garlic noodles to warm serving bowls, top with the spiced shrimp mixture, and serve immediately, garnished with the remaining cilantro.

SPICY ORANGE NOODLES WITH SEARED SCALLOPS

SERVES: 4　　　**PREP TIME: 10 MINS**　　　**COOK TIME: 10 MINS**

INGREDIENTS

12 ounces fresh udon noodles

12–16 scallops, corals removed

1 tablespoon unsalted butter

1 tablespoon olive oil

salt and pepper, to taste

3 scallions, thinly sliced, to garnish

DRESSING

3 garlic cloves, finely chopped

1 tablespoon finely chopped fresh ginger

zest and juice of 1 orange

¼ cup soy sauce

⅓ cup sweet chili sauce

½ cup vegetable oil

1. Cook the noodles according to the package directions. Drain and set aside.

2. To make the dressing, combine the garlic, ginger, orange zest and juice, soy sauce, and sweet chili sauce in a bowl and whisk to combine. Add the oil and whisk until emulsified.

3. Rinse the scallops, pat them dry, and season with salt and pepper. Heat the butter and oil in a large skillet over high heat until the butter has melted. Add the scallops and sear for about 1½ minutes on each side, until they have a golden-brown crust but are still translucent in the center.

4. In a large bowl, toss the noodles with most of the dressing. Divide the noodles among four plates. Top each with three or four scallops. Drizzle a little more dressing over the scallops and serve immediately, garnished with scallions.

HERO TIPS

To cook perfect scallops, make sure your pan is particularly hot and your scallops are dry before cooking.

SINGAPORE NOODLES

SERVES: 4 **PREP TIME: 15 MINS** **COOK TIME: 15 MINS**

INGREDIENTS

8 ounces fine rice noodles

1 tablespoon mild, medium, or hot curry paste, to taste

1 teaspoon ground turmeric

⅓ cup water

2 tablespoons peanut oil or corn oil

½ onion, thinly sliced

2 large garlic cloves, thinly sliced

1 cup small broccoli florets

1 cup green beans (1-inch pieces)

4 ounces pork tenderloin, cut into thin strips

4 ounces small cooked, peeled shrimp, thawed if frozen

1 cup thinly shredded Chinese greens or romaine lettuce

1 fresh Thai chile, seeded and thinly sliced

2 scallions, white parts only, thinly shredded

fresh cilantro, to garnish

1. Prepare the noodles according to the package directions. Drain and set aside. Meanwhile, put the curry paste and turmeric in a small bowl and stir in ¼ cup of the water, then set aside.

2. Heat a wok over high heat, then add the oil. Add the onion and garlic and stir-fry for 1 minute, or until the onion softens. Add the broccoli and beans to the wok with the remaining water and continue stir-frying for 2 minutes. Add the pork and stir-fry for an additional minute. Add the shrimp, Chinese greens, and chile to the wok and continue stir-frying for an additional 2 minutes, until the pork is cooked through and the vegetables are tender but still with a little bite. Remove from the wok and keep warm.

3. Add the scallions, noodles, and curry paste mixture to the wok. Use two forks to mix together the noodles and onions, and continue stir-frying for about 2 minutes, until the noodles are hot and have picked up a dark golden color from the turmeric. Return the other ingredients to the wok and continue stir-frying for 1 minute. Serve immediately, garnished with fresh cilantro.

SPICY SHRIMP IN A RAMEN NOODLE NEST

A crispy noodle nest makes the perfect backdrop for succulent shrimp bathed in a sweet, spicy sauce.

SERVES: 4

PREP TIME: 5 MINS, PLUS CHILLING

COOK TIME: 10 MINS

INGREDIENTS

2 tablespoons Chinese rice wine or dry sherry

1 tablespoon cornstarch

¼ teaspoon salt

1½ pounds peeled and deveined raw shrimp

12 ounces dried ramen noodles (flavoring envelope discarded, if included)

2 tablespoons vegetable oil, plus extra for deep-frying

3 tablespoons chicken stock

2 tablespoons ketchup

1 tablespoon oyster sauce

1 tablespoon soy sauce

1 tablespoon chili paste

2 garlic cloves, finely chopped

1 tablespoon finely chopped fresh ginger

4 scallions, thinly sliced

1. Whisk together the wine, cornstarch, and salt in a medium bowl. Add the shrimp and toss to coat. Cover and chill in the refrigerator for 15 minutes.

2. Meanwhile, cook the noodles according to the package directions. Drain and spread out on a clean dish towel to dry. Transfer to a baking sheet and shape into a large nest that will fit into a skillet. Place the baking sheet in the freezer for about 20 minutes. Line a plate with paper towels.

3. To cook the noodle nest, pour 2 inches of oil into a deep skillet and heat until hot. Carefully slide the frozen noodle nest into the hot oil and cook for 1 minute, or until golden brown. Transfer to the prepared plate.

4. Whisk together the stock, ketchup, oyster sauce, soy sauce, and chili paste in a small bowl.

5. Heat 1 tablespoon of the oil in a large, nonstick skillet over medium–high heat. Add the shrimp and cook, stirring frequently, until opaque and cooked through. Remove the shrimp from the pan.

6. In the same pan, heat the remaining tablespoon of oil over medium–high heat. Add the garlic and ginger and cook, stirring, for about 2 minutes, until fragrant. Add the sauce mixture and cook until the sauce bubbles and thickens. Return the shrimp to the pan along with the scallions. Cook, stirring, for an additional 2 minutes, until the sauce is thick and the shrimp are heated through.

7. Transfer the noodle nest to a serving plate and spoon the shrimp and sauce into it. Serve immediately, using a spatula to cut the nest into wedges so that each diner gets some crispy noodles along with the shrimp.

SALMON WITH SOBA NOODLES & SWISS CHARD

SERVES: 4   **PREP TIME: 10 MINS**   **COOK TIME: 20 MINS**

INGREDIENTS

6 garlic cloves, thinly sliced

¼ cup water

¼ cup Chinese rice wine or sake

¼ cup sugar

1 tablespoon unsalted butter

juice of 1 lime

2 teaspoons finely chopped fresh ginger

2 teaspoons curry powder

¼ –½ teaspoon cayenne pepper

¼ cup olive oil

4 salmon fillets (about 6 ounces each)

½ teaspoon pepper

12 ounces soba noodles

1 bunch of Swiss chard, main stems removed and leaves julienned

¼ cup chopped fresh cilantro

salt

1. Combine the garlic, water, wine, sugar, and butter in a small saucepan. Bring to a simmer and cook, stirring frequently, for 6–8 minutes, until the mixture is syrupy. Remove from the heat and stir in the lime juice.

2. Combine the ginger, curry powder, cayenne pepper, and 2 tablespoons of the oil. Season the salmon with a pinch of salt and the pepper and brush with the spice mixture.

3. Cook the noodles according to the package directions, drain, and transfer to a large bowl.

4. Heat 1 tablespoon of the oil in a large skillet over medium–high heat. Add the Swiss chard and a pinch of salt and cook, stirring frequently, for 2–3 minutes, until tender. Transfer the chard to the bowl with the noodles and toss to combine.

5. Heat the remaining oil in the same pan. Cook the fish for 3–4 minutes on each side, until nicely seared on the outside and just barely pink in the center.

6. Divide the noodles among four bowls, top each with a fish fillet, and drizzle the garlic syrup over them, along with several slices of the garlic. Serve immediately, garnished with cilantro.

SHRIMP NOODLE BOWL

This hearty meal-in-a-bowl is packed with delicious Thai-style flavors.

SERVES: 4   **PREP TIME: 10 MINS**   **COOK TIME: 8-10 MINS**

INGREDIENTS

8 ounces rice noodles

2 tablespoons peanut oil

½ cup unsalted peanuts

1 bunch of scallions, diagonally sliced

2 celery stalks, trimmed and diagonally sliced

1 red bell pepper, seeded and thinly sliced

1 fresh Thai chile, sliced

1 lemongrass stalk, crushed

1¾ cups fish stock or chicken stock

1 cup coconut milk

2 teaspoons Thai fish sauce

12 ounces cooked, peeled jumbo shrimp

3 tablespoons chopped fresh cilantro, to garnish

1. Prepare the noodles according to the package directions. Drain and set aside.

2. Heat a wok over medium–high heat, then add the oil. Add the peanuts and stir-fry for 1–2 minutes, until golden. Remove with a slotted spoon.

3. Add the scallions, celery, and red bell pepper and stir-fry over high heat for 1–2 minutes.

4. Add the chile, lemongrass, stock, coconut milk, and fish sauce and bring to a boil. Stir in the shrimp, then return to a boil, stirring. Stir in the noodles.

5. Serve immediately, garnished with the cilantro and toasted peanuts.

GARLIC UDON NOODLES WITH CRABMEAT

These super-garlicky noodles, topped with succulent crabmeat and an unexpected touch of Parmesan cheese, make a fantastic quick dinner or late-night snack.

SERVES: 4　　　　**PREP TIME: 5 MINS**　　　　**COOK TIME: 10 MINS**

INGREDIENTS

1 pound fresh udon noodles
6 tablespoons unsalted butter
6 garlic cloves, finely chopped
6 scallions, thinly sliced
1 tablespoon oyster sauce
1 tablespoon soy sauce
1 tablespoon sugar
3 (6-ounce) cans crabmeat
¼ cup freshly grated
Parmesan cheese, to garnish

1. Cook the noodles according to the package directions. Drain and set aside.

2. Melt the butter in a saucepan over medium–high heat. Add the garlic and scallions and cook, stirring, for 1 minute. Add the oyster sauce, soy sauce and sugar and cook, stirring, for an additional minute.

3. Add the noodles and toss to coat well. Remove from the heat and stir in the crabmeat. Serve hot, garnished with Parmesan cheese.

HERO TIPS

You can also use fresh dressed crabmeat in this dish. Use a mixture of both white and dark meat for a richer, fuller flavor.

VEG OUT

RAMEN WITH BOK CHOY & TOFU

This simple, but richly flavored soup makes a quick and satisfying vegetarian meal. Barbecuing the bok choy and tofu adds an intriguing layer of smokiness to the dish.

SERVES: 4

PREP TIME: 10 MINS, PLUS SOAKING

COOK TIME: 40 MINS

INGREDIENTS

12 ounces extra firm tofu, cut into 1-inch-thick slices

½ ounce dried shiitake mushrooms

6⅓ cups vegetable stock

⅓ cup soy sauce

1 tablespoon sake or dry white wine

4-inch piece fresh ginger, peeled and sliced

¼ cup rice vinegar

4 teaspoons sesame oil

12 ounces bok choy, halved or quartered lengthwise

1 tablespoon honey

8 ounces fresh shiitake mushrooms

12 ounces dried ramen noodles (flavoring envelope discarded, if included)

4 scallions, thinly sliced, to garnish

1. Place the tofu slices in a single layer on a large baking sheet lined with a clean dish towel. Top with another clean dish towel. Place a second baking sheet on top and weigh it down with heavy dishes or cans of food to squeeze as much moisture from the tofu as possible. Set aside for 30 minutes.

2. Meanwhile, soak the dried mushrooms in hot water for 30 minutes. Drain, reserving the liquid, and slice the mushrooms.

3. Combine the stock, ¼ cup of the soy sauce, the sake, mushroom soaking water, ginger, 1 tablespoon of the vinegar, and 1 teaspoon of the sesame oil in a medium saucepan. Bring to a simmer over medium heat. Reduce the heat to low and simmer for about 15 minutes. Remove and discard the ginger slices. Add the reserved soaked mushrooms and simmer for an additional 15 minutes, or until the mushrooms are tender.

4. Meanwhile, preheat the grill or broiler to medium. Place the bok choy in a microwave-safe dish, cover, and cook in the microwave on high for about 3 minutes. Whisk together the remaining vinegar, the remaining soy sauce, the honey, and

the remaining sesame oil in a large bowl. Brush the tofu all over with the sauce, then add the bok choy and fresh mushrooms to the bowl and toss to coat well. Place the tofu and vegetables on the grill or broiler rack and cook for about 2 minutes on each side, until nicely charred and tender. Brush with any remaining sauce. Slice the tofu into 2-inch-wide strips.

5. Bring the soup back to a boil. Add the noodles and cook, breaking them up with a spoon, for 3 minutes, or until tender. Stir in the scallions. Serve immediately, topped with the tofu and vegetables.

HOT & SOUR NOODLES WITH TOFU

SERVES: 4   **PREP TIME: 15 MINS**   **COOK TIME: 20 MINS**

INGREDIENTS

3 strips lime zest

2 garlic cloves, peeled

2 slices fresh ginger

4¼ cups chicken stock

1 tablespoon vegetable oil

6 ounces firm tofu, cubed

8 ounces dried fine egg noodles

4 ounces shiitake mushrooms, sliced

1 fresh red chile, seeded and sliced

4 scallions, sliced

1 teaspoon soy sauce

juice of 1 lime

1 teaspoon Chinese rice wine

1 teaspoon sesame oil

chopped fresh cilantro, to garnish

1. Put the lime zest, garlic, and ginger into a large saucepan with the stock and bring to a boil. Reduce the heat and simmer for 5 minutes. Remove the lime zest, garlic, and ginger with a slotted spoon and discard.

2. Meanwhile, heat the vegetable oil in a large skillet over high heat, add the tofu, and cook, turning frequently, until golden. Remove from the pan and drain on paper towels.

3. Add the noodles, mushrooms, and chile to the stock and simmer for 3 minutes. Add the tofu, scallions, soy sauce, lime juice, rice wine, and sesame oil and briefly heat through.

4. Divide among four warm bowls, sprinkle with the cilantro, and serve immediately.

MUSHROOM & TOFU LAKSA WITH NOODLES

SERVES: 4 **PREP TIME: 15 MINS** **COOK TIME: 10 MINS**

INGREDIENTS

3½ cups vegetable stock

1¾ cups coconut milk

8 ounces shiitake mushrooms, stems removed, thinly sliced

6 ounces firm tofu, cubed

2 tablespoons tomato paste

6 ounces fine egg noodles

salt and pepper, to taste

8 scallions, sliced, and ¼ cup shredded mint leaves, to garnish

SPICE PASTE

2 red chiles, seeded and chopped

1½-inch piece fresh ginger, chopped

2 large garlic cloves, chopped

2 lemongrass stalks, tough outer layers discarded, inner stalks chopped

1 teaspoon coriander seeds, crushed

6 macadamia nuts, chopped

small handful of cilantro leaves

3 tablespoons vegetable oil

1. Put the spice paste ingredients into a food processor or blender and process until smooth.

2. Heat a wok over medium–high heat, add the spice paste, and stir-fry for 30 seconds. Pour in the stock and coconut milk and bring to a boil. Add the mushrooms, tofu, and tomato paste and season with salt and pepper. Simmer gently for 5 minutes.

3. Cook the noodles according to the package directions.

4. Divide among four warm soup bowls and ladle the spicy tofu broth over the noodles. Serve immediately, garnished with scallions and mint leaves.

SOBA NOODLE SALAD

A Japanese-inspired salad made with just-cooked soba noodles tossed in a tamari and ginger dressing and speckled with nutrient-boosting broccoli and protein-packed edamame (soybeans).

SERVES: 4   **PREP TIME: 15 MINS**   **COOK TIME: 10 MINS**

INGREDIENTS

6 ounces soba noodles

1⅓ cups frozen edamame (soybeans)

3 cups small broccoli florets and thinly sliced stems

1 red bell pepper, halved, seeded, and thinly sliced

1 purple or orange bell pepper, halved, seeded, and thinly sliced

2 cups thinly sliced cremini mushrooms

¾ cup sunflower sprouts

DRESSING

2 tablespoons rice vinegar

2 tablespoons tamari (Japanese soy sauce)

¼ cup rice bran oil

1½-inch piece of fresh ginger, peeled and finely grated

1. Put cold water in the bottom of a steamer, bring to a boil, then add the noodles and frozen edamame (soybeans) and bring back to a boil. Put the broccoli in the top of the steamer, then put it on the steamer base, cover, and steam for 3–5 minutes, or until the noodles and vegetables are just tender. Drain and rinse the noodles and edamame, then drain again and transfer to a salad bowl. Add the broccoli, then let cool.

2. To make the dressing, put the vinegar, tamari, oil, and ginger in a screw-top jar, screw on the lid, and shake well. Drizzle the dressing over the salad and toss gently together.

3. Add both bell peppers and the mushrooms and toss again. Spoon into bowls, top with the sprouts, and serve immediately.

NOODLE NUTRITION
(THE HEALTH BENEFITS OF NOODLES)

Noodles are a staple part of the diet in many cultures across the world. They are naturally low in fat and a good source of starchy carbohydrate and the whole-wheat versions are rich in dietary fiber. Because noodles tend to contain added salt, there's no need to add salt to the cooking water.

One of the biggest benefits of eating noodles—apart from their speed in cooking—is their ability to easily take on other flavors, making them the perfect pantry ingredient.

They can form the basis of a substantial meal that's ready in minutes and pair with other food groups perfectly, from fish, meat, chicken, or vegetarian meat alternatives, such as tofu.

Soba

Soba noodles, which are made from pure buckwheat (check the packaging for exact content because it varies) are ideal for those intolerant and avoiding wheat and gluten. The buckwheat used in soba noodles contains about 12-15 percent protein, including the essential amino acid lysine, which isn't present in most cereal grains. It also contains lipids, iron, phosphorous, copper, and vitamins B_1 and B_2.

Choline, another important micronutrient found in buckwheat, plays an important role in our metabolism, particularly regulating blood pressure and liver function.

Udon

Carbohydrate makes up the major nutrient found in udon, and it's this that converts to glucose and glycogen in the body. Glycogen becomes both a physical and mental energy source. Compared to pasta and some other foods, udon is digested quickly, and rapidly becomes a source of energy for the brain and body. Udon can possibly aid increased performance when concentration is needed. It might be said that it's well suited for lunch as a healthy afternoon energy source.

Tests have shown that udon is digested at three times the speed of beef, making it especially suitable for people who have colds and or weakened digestive function.

Rice

Rice noodles made from white rice flour are a great alternative to those made from wheat and perfect for

anyone avoiding wheat and gluten due to sensitivity or celiac disease.

Rice noodles are a good source of phosphorus, which is the second most abundant mineral in the body. Phosphorus is responsible for strengthening bones and teeth and also assists in filtering out waste in the kidneys, as well as helping the body store, process, and use energy.

Egg

As well as being a good source of medium-density carbohydrates, these noodles contain similar levels of protein to whole eggs, due to the egg content.

SOBA NOODLES WITH A HONEY-SOY DRESSING

This simple salad, made with fresh edamame (soybeans), makes a wonderful light meal on a warm evening, or a great dish for a picnic.

SERVES: 4   **PREP TIME: 10 MINS**   **COOK TIME: 10 MINS**

INGREDIENTS

8 ounces dried soba noodles
2 cups shredded cabbage
2 carrots, shredded
1 cup fresh edamame (soybeans), shelled and blanched
4 scallions, thinly sliced
2 tablespoons toasted sesame seeds, to garnish

DRESSING

3 tablespoons low-sodium soy sauce
2 tablespoons rice wine vinegar
1 tablespoon honey
1 teaspoon sesame oil

1. Cook the noodles according to the package directions. Drain, rinse well with cold water, and set aside to cool completely.

2. To make the dressing, whisk together the soy sauce, vinegar, honey, and oil in a small bowl.

3. Combine the noodles, cabbage, carrots, edamame (soybeans), and scallions in a large bowl and toss to mix well. Add the dressing and toss again to combine. Serve immediately, garnished with toasted sesame seeds.

HERO TIPS

This delicious and hearty salad will keep well for up to three days in the refrigerator.

TEMPEH NOODLE BOWL

Tempeh has an even higher protein content than tofu and is naturally cholesterol-free.

SERVES: 4 **PREP TIME: 10 MINS** **COOK TIME: 7-10 MINS**

INGREDIENTS

4 ounces shiitake mushrooms

2 tablespoons miso paste

2½ cups boiling water

3 cups diagonally halved snow peas

8 ounces tempeh or smoked tofu, cubed

1 bunch scallions, sliced

6 ounces dried udon or soba noodles

1. Remove the stems from the mushrooms and cut a deep cross in the top of the caps.

2. Place the miso and water in a large saucepan and stir thoroughly to dissolve the miso. Place the pan over high heat and bring back to a boil. Add the mushrooms and snow peas and cook for 2–3 minutes to soften. Stir the tempeh and scallions into the pan and cook for another 2 minutes.

3. Meanwhile, cook the noodles according to the package directions, then divide among four warm bowls.

4. Spoon the tempeh and vegetable mixture over the noodles and serve immediately.

HERO TIPS

To clean your shiitake mushrooms, simply wipe over with a damp piece of paper towel. Washing mushrooms exposes them to too much water and can leave them soggy and unappetizing.

NOODLE STIR-FRY

This recipe is fantastically quick, easy, and simple, making it an ideal choice when you have little time on your hands but still want a delicious meal.

SERVES: 2   **PREP TIME: 10 MINS**   **COOK TIME: 10 MINS**

INGREDIENTS

5 ounces flat rice noodles

3 tablespoons soy sauce

2 tablespoons lemon juice

1 teaspoon granulated sugar

½ teaspoon cornstarch

1 tablespoon vegetable oil

2 teaspoons grated fresh ginger

2 garlic cloves, chopped

4–5 scallions, trimmed and sliced

2 tablespoons rice wine or dry sherry

1 (8-ounce) can water chestnuts, drained and sliced

1. Prepare the noodles according to the package directions. Drain and set aside.

2. Mix together the soy sauce, lemon juice, sugar, and cornstarch in a small bowl. Set aside.

3. Heat a wok over medium–high heat, then add the oil. Add the ginger and garlic and stir-fry for 1 minute. Add the scallions and stir-fry for 3 minutes.

4. Add the rice wine, then add the soy sauce mixture and cook for 1 minute.

5. Stir in the water chestnuts and noodles and cook for an additional 1–2 minutes, or until heated through. Serve immediately.

RAMEN NOODLE CAKES

A handful of ingredients turns a package of ramen noodles into a quick, satisfying dinner or a scrumptious late-night snack. This is delicious served with a cucumber-yogurt dip.

SERVES: 4   **PREP TIME: 5 MINS**   **COOK TIME: 10 MINS**

INGREDIENTS

6 ounces dried ramen noodles (flavoring envelope discarded, if included)

4 eggs, lightly beaten

3 cups shredded cabbage

1 large carrot, shredded

4 scallions, thinly sliced

½ cup medium curry paste

3 tablespoons all-purpose flour

1–2 tablespoons vegetable oil

1. Cook the noodles according to the package directions for about 2 minutes. Drain, rinse with cold water, and drain well again.

2. Combine the eggs, cabbage, carrot, scallions, curry paste, and flour in a large bowl and mix well. Add the drained noodles and stir to combine.

3. Heat the oil in a large skillet over medium–high heat. Add the noodle mixture, ¼ cup at a time. Use the back of a ladle or spoon to flatten each pancake as you add it to the pan. Cook for about 2 minutes on each side, until nicely browned and beginning to crisp. Serve hot.

HERO TIPS

Quick-cooking ramen noodles make this recipe lightning-fast to make, but any noodles could be substituted successfully.

SICHUAN NOODLES

SERVES: 4   **PREP TIME: 10 MINS**   **COOK TIME: 8–10 MINS**

INGREDIENTS

8 ounces thick egg noodles

2 tablespoons peanut oil or corn oil

2 large garlic cloves, minced

1 large red onion, cut in half and thinly sliced

½ cup vegetable stock or water

2 tablespoons chili bean sauce

2 tablespoons Chinese sesame paste

1 tablespoon dried Sichuan peppercorns, roasted and ground

1 teaspoon light soy sauce

2 small bok choy or other Chinese cabbage, cut into quarters

1 large carrot, shredded

1. Prepare the noodles according to the package directions. Drain and set aside.

2. Heat a wok over high heat and add the oil. Add the garlic and onion and stir-fry for 1 minute.

3. Add the vegetable stock, chili bean sauce, sesame paste, ground Sichuan peppercorns, and soy sauce and bring to a boil, stirring to blend the ingredients together.

4. Add the bok choy quarters and shredded carrot and continue to stir-fry for 1–2 minutes, until they are just wilted. Add the noodles and continue stir-frying.

5. Using two forks, mix all the ingredients together until the noodles are hot. Transfer to bowls and serve immediately.

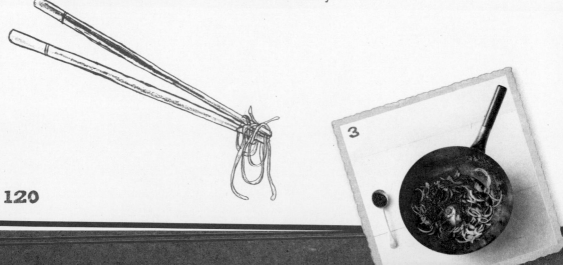

SPICY VEGETABLE & TOFU UDON NOODLES

This is one of those magical dishes where a few simple ingredients transform themselves into a delectable meal in minutes.

SERVES: 4   **PREP TIME: 5 MINS**   **COOK TIME: 15 MINS**

INGREDIENTS

2 cups green beans (1-inch pieces)

2 tablespoons water

2 tablespoons sriracha

2 tablespoons rice vinegar

2 tablespoons soy sauce

12 ounces dried udon noodles

1 tablespoon vegetable oil

1 tablespoon sesame oil

2½ garlic cloves, finely chopped

8 ounces extra firm tofu, cut into 1-inch cubes

8 cups baby spinach

2 tablespoons toasted sesame seeds, to garnish

1. Place the green beans in a microwave-safe bowl with the water. Cover and microwave on high for 2 minutes, then drain.

2. Stir together the sriracha, vinegar, and soy sauce in a small bowl.

3. Cook the noodles according to the package directions. Drain and set aside.

4. Meanwhile, heat the vegetable oil and sesame oil in a large skillet over medium–high heat. Add the garlic and cook, stirring, for 1 minute. Add the tofu and green beans and cook, stirring occasionally, for 1 minute, until the green beans are tender and the tofu is beginning to brown. Stir in the spinach and cook for 2 minutes, until it wilts. Add the noodles and sauce mixture and toss to combine well.

5. Serve immediately, garnished with toasted sesame seeds.

CRISPY NOODLES WITH BOK CHOY

Lightly cooked bok choy and deep-fried crunchy noodles are a simple but stylish combination.

SERVES: 4   **PREP TIME: 10 MINS**   **COOK TIME: 8-10 MINS**

INGREDIENTS

2 tablespoons peanut oil, plus extra for deep-frying

4 ounces dried rice vermicelli

1 tablespoon crushed palm sugar or brown sugar

1 tablespoon rice vinegar

1 tablespoon Thai fish sauce

1 tablespoon lime juice

6 scallions, sliced

1 garlic clove, thinly sliced

12 ounces small bok choy, quartered lengthwise

3 tablespoons oyster sauce

sesame seeds, to sprinkle

1. Heat enough oil for deep-frying in a large saucepan to 350–375°F, or until a cube of bread browns in 30 seconds. Add the noodles, in batches, and fry for 15–20 seconds, until puffed and golden. Drain on paper towels.

2. Heat the sugar, vinegar, fish sauce, and lime juice in a small saucepan until the sugar dissolves. Boil for 20–30 seconds until syrupy.

3. Heat 2 tablespoons of the oil in a wok and stir-fry the scallions and garlic for 1 minute. Add the bok choy and stir-fry for 2–3 minutes. Stir in the oyster sauce.

4. Toss the noodles with the syrup and the bok choy. Serve the dish immediately, sprinkled with sesame seeds.

UDON NOODLES WITH KALE & MISO

This simple, nutritious, and filling dish is comfort food at its best. Add some broiled tofu for added protein, if you desire.

SERVES: 4   **PREP TIME: 10 MINS**   **COOK TIME: 25 MINS**

INGREDIENTS

2 tablespoons olive oil

1 large red onion, halved and thinly sliced

½ teaspoon salt

1 tablespoon Chinese black rice vinegar or balsamic vinegar

12 ounces dried udon noodles

2 garlic cloves, finely chopped

12 ounces kale

2 tablespoons white miso paste

¼ cup Chinese rice wine or mirin

¼ cup water

2 tablespoons rice vinegar

1 tablespoon unsalted butter

2 tablespoons toasted sesame seeds, to garnish

1. Heat 1 tablespoon of the oil in a large skillet over medium–high heat. Add the onions and ¼ teaspoon of the salt, reduce the heat to medium–low, and cook, stirring occasionally, for 15–20 minutes, until the onions are soft and beginning to turn golden. Remove from the heat and stir in the black rice vinegar.

2. Meanwhile, cook the noodles according to the package directions. Drain and transfer to a large bowl.

3. Transfer the cooked onions to a bowl. Add the remaining oil to the pan and heat over medium–high heat. Add the garlic and cook, stirring, for 1 minute. Add the kale with the remaining salt and cook, stirring frequently, for 4 minutes, until wilted. Remove from the heat.

4. Combine the miso paste, wine, water, and rice vinegar in a small saucepan and bring to a boil over medium–high heat, stirring constantly until the miso is fully incorporated. Reduce the heat to

medium–low and simmer for 2–3 minutes, until the sauce thickens. Remove from the heat and immediately stir in the butter until it has completely melted. Add the sauce to the noodles and toss well.

5. Serve the noodles in small bowls. Arrange some of the kale in a pile on top, with a pile of the onions alongside. Garnish with the sesame seeds and serve immediately.

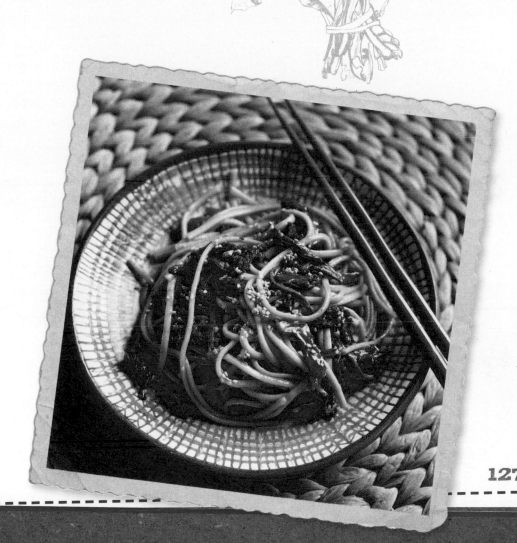

Index